Prayers
and Verses
for Contemplation

Prayers
and Verses
for contemplation

by Evelyn Francis Capel

Floris Books

First published in 1992 by Floris Books
© Evelyn Francis Capel, 1992
All rights reserved. No part of this publication
may be reproduced without the permission of
Floris Books, 15 Harrison Gardens, Edinburgh

British Library CIP Data available

ISBN 0–86315–133–7

Printed in Great Britain
by Billing & Sons, Worcester

Contents

Introduction

It is time to begin again. The past has reached a pause and a new effort is required. This is true quite specially of what is aimed at in our inner life of meditation and prayer. The old form of prayer became a process of asking: asking for all that which a person feels he requires for a satisfactory way of living. The new form of prayer is making the effort to find what is within my being which will make known to me the answer that is already there.

Can it be imagined that Christ does not know about human need, that he has not already brought into the world what a Christian soul can use? The act of praying wakens the mind and heart to discovery of what is here and challenges the human will to go out and realize it. An illustration to this thought is found in the story in St Luke's Gospel of the shepherds in the field on Christmas night. They were awake when others were asleep. The door of heaven opened and the angels sang to them about the birth of the Child. Listening, their hearts were opened to understand. Understanding, they followed the advice of the angel and found the way to Bethlehem. They encountered the true fact of Christmas and they went around spreading the news among their friends and neighbours, who had been asleep when the angels sang. They found what was given to them from the heavens and they celebrated what they knew.

Prayer has been for a long while reciting and requesting. In Shakespeare's *Hamlet*, there is a description of how prayer should change, but it has been given in a speech made by the uncle of Hamlet, who had murdered his brother in order to become king. In his woe, he wishes to pray, but he becomes conscious of his words not reaching beyond himself to the ear of God. His thoughts are not finding an answer in the words, because they are being dragged down to the situation he is in on earth and which he himself has produced. Prayer begins with the thoughts of moral meaning which live in the heart before words can bring the answer. In an earlier time, when repeating words was in itself an achievement, such a discovery about prayer could not have been made. But because the struggles of Hamlet and the people around him were connected with a new kind of consciousness, which prepared the change experienced today, a discovery about prayer is needed. It begins with finding the answer in the thoughts within, rather than making requests. The responsibility becomes human for the task of finding a new faith in God.

Inner and Outer Life

In the Communion Service of the Christian Community, the Act of Consecration of Man, a vestment is worn by the celebrant which is called the chasuble. On the front, facing the altar, the design appears of the figure of eight, also called the lemniscate. It represents two circles, one above and one below, interweaving so that there is a crossing point at the centre. The design represents the heavenly world interweaving with the earthly. It can likewise be read to represent Man as a being of spirit living in a body of flesh. The design speaks also of what a spiritually minded person has as his aim when he intends to care for his inner life in the midst of all the pressing interests that make their demands in the outer life.

In the course of the year, under the influence of those heavenly beings called the archangels who revolve the seasons, a time that is holy by nature is reached every year at Christmas. During the twelve holy nights the frontier between heaven and earth is opened; cosmic forces flow into the life of the human soul. The door of heaven stands open. In the interchange of day and night, that is to say of sleeping and waking, there is also a holy moment just as one goes to sleep, and likewise as one wakes up. The soul is poised between heaven and earth, between the inner impulses of the spirit and the pressures of the outer world. Such holy moments are provided. All too easily they can be disregarded. If they are rightly apprehended they are opportunities for the spiritual life to come into its own within the rhythms of daily life.

The first requirement for using these gifts of the arch-angels is quiet attention, to be quiet within and yet to be awake. Quiet can be active. It is important to keep the outer problems away without forgetting them or ignoring one's sense of responsibility. It is all too easy to take the line that one will feel quiet when the outer duties are finished. This method leads to illusion. One outer duty leads to another. Only the conviction, which is made stronger and stronger, that the inner requirements are just as real as the outer ones, and should have their due, can help a person to give proper time and thought to his inner life. Today we cope with an outlook among the people around us which makes only the outer things shareable. Conversation and interest between people is usually directed towards something outside. The courtesies of the inner life are not readily understood. One friend living in the country found that her neighbours considered it bad taste to speak about inner experiences or matters of religion at a tea party.

Sharing that which belongs to the inner and spiritual life is something most important to be studied and under-stood. If one's inner life is made entirely private, it is in danger of becoming egotistical, just as if it were entirely externalized it would become a matter of form. The affairs of one's inner life require time and attention if they are to grow. They also require a space in one's outer affairs that they may not become over-personal. Skill in managing one's time and one's interests becomes an important part in the effort to protect one's inner life from being over-whelmed by the outer.

Sharing the inner life means exchange of thought, common study and ritual through which each one can have a spiritual experience in the presence of others. Caring for one's own inner life means time and attention given to thought, prayer and meditation.

The natural time to give attention to one's personal inner life is on going to sleep and again on awakening. The middle of the day may also be marked with a form of prayer. It is of value to keep oneself free to make one's own choice of form for prayer and meditation. To follow a pattern laid down by an authority outside oneself is of lesser value, as that would mean avoiding one's own responsibility. If one feels that one makes mistakes, the opportunity is there to learn by experience. It is a pity to suppose that one should follow expert advice. In modern times, that which is most important is to bring one's inner life into relationship to one's own true self, into the sphere of egohood. This has more value than being right or relying on authority from outside. Only when the individual Spirit within is active and accepts its own decisions will that part of the soul be awakened which can pray. Not the prayers prescribed by the right authority, but the rightly prayed prayers are important.

The natural time for ritual, that is to say in The Christian Community for the sacrament of Communion, the Act of Consecration, is in the morning before noon. The further sacraments are less related to the time of day. Why should this be? Is it not more convenient for people to attend a service in the evening or late afternoon? The difference between morning and afternoon is a cosmic one. While the sun is rising to its height, the relationship between the earth and the starry heavens is different from that part of the day when the sun is declining towards sunset. While the sun is in the process of rising the spiritual forces created in the celebration of the Act of Consecration of Man can stream out towards the starry heavens. There

11

they are received into the weaving of cosmic forces created among the angels, archangels and all the company of heaven. Powers rising from Man's life on earth are offered to the divine world. There is giving and receiving, coming and going from earth to heaven, from heaven to earth. It is the work of Christ that this is so. When he overcame death, the door of heaven was opened and stands open still that we human souls may receive and may offer.

Where would the flowers be
Without the dancing of the stars?
Where would the stones be
Without the flowing down of forms?
Where would the beast be
Without the guiding light of sun and moon?
How would the earth exist
Without the heavens?
What would become of the heavens
Without the earth?
How would Mankind progress
Without the love of God?
What would become of God
Without Man?
What would become of Man
Without the Son of God?

Pictures from the Apocalypse

The Garden and the City

God planted the garden,
He nourished the growth,
Giving birth to Man's form
In the temple of earth.

He walked in the garden
In the glory of light,
Clothing Man's form
With the grace of his life.

God called in the serpent
To hide in the tree,
Handing out apples
That with poison set free.

Exchanging the garden
For the dark world instead,
Who is strong in the vision
Of what shines far ahead?

We walking in shadow
Where death's hand wields with might,
We labour at building
God's city of light.

From the gold of the Sun
Shining heart–felt above,
Stones for the building
Are fashioned in love.

The Spirit of God

The wide dominions of heaven
Are thy dwelling,
Wherein thou art reigning
Over the ninefold company
Of those who heed thy bidding.

In the immensities of thy wisdom
Thou containest those who oppose,
That good shall not exclude evil,
That nothing is destroyed,
Not the work of the Devil.

For thy arms are outstretched
To uphold from beneath
That which is above.
That the wide world be kept
In thy lasting love.

In the round of eternities
Thou art the beating heart
That the universals shall not cease
Releasing time–driven souls
Into thy lasting peace.

Behold with thy endless compassion
Our sadly struggling souls
From the risk of temptation
Lead us into thy divine presence
On the way of salvation.

The Risen One

Into deeps of despair,
Into black of the dark
Didst thou descend
Champion of light.

Through dread of sin,
Through doom of self,
Didst thou stride on
Champion of life.

Into light out of death,
Into light out of dark
Didst thou arise
Saviour from evil.

In life resurrected,
In light new created
Didst thou come forth
Saviour of Man.

The Seed and the Fruit

The sun has sown a seed
In the dark of the earth.
Its radiance shines,
In the depths, a new birth.

The seed of life fell down
Into the place of death.
It quickens the dead to life,
Breathing with living breath.

The fruit grows from the flower
In the light of the sun;
The treasure of seed within
Shall ripen for time to come.

The Book

The Book of Life is kept in heaven,
On earth the Book of Death.
Who writes therein but we ourselves,
Deciding what our scheme is worth,
In deeds and words of good and life,
Or those of baleful bad and death.
Who judges? We ourselves on earth,
The voice of God will judge in heaven.

The Redeemed

In shining white they go
Who bore the test of tribulation
Who glow with joy of jubilation
Who walk in high anticipation
To the throne set up in heaven.

The sounds of earth–bred song
Shall precede their great procession.
They shall greet the high occasion
With distinctive diapason
Which they alone sent forth from earth can sing.

War in Heaven

Who fought in heaven?
War is not heaven's affair.
Are not the heavenly fields
Divinely calm and fair?
Nowhere shall right and good
Prevail as there.
How can the world proceed
Bereft of God's care?

Who fights in heaven?
He on a wild rampage,
He in a dragon's rage.
He stormed in heaven about,
He called his angels out.
Michael took up his sword
God's peace in heaven to guard.
He threw the dragon far
Down to a distant star.

Earth receives him down below,
Earth receives him to our woe.
Who will bind him?
Who will put him down
Under our feet below?
The champion of Christ calls his angels,
Calls his human companions,
Calls his heroes to heroism.

Christ Becoming Man

Man descended,
Christ descending.
Man benighted,
Christ enlightening.
Man bedevilled,
Christ befriending.
Man downfallen,
Christ uprising.
Man polluted,
Christ him cleansing.
Man earthbounded,
Christ releasing.
Man beleaguered,
Christ him succouring.
Man dead–stricken,
Christ upraising.
Man bewildered,
Christ him guiding.
Man lost to purpose,
Christ onward pointing
On to the City of God
Far, far ahead.

The Archangel Michael

Sun–born,
Star–bred,
Heaven–sent,
Earth free.
You despoil the dragon,
You dispel his might.
Down he must slide,
Down into the night.

Heaven–born,
Spirit–bred,
Christ chosen
Guard to keep.
You summon Mankind,
You beckon aright.
Up rises Man's soul
Up from dark to the light.

The City

Sunwards
Lightwards
Heavenwards we go.

Are we far on the road?
Shadows so drear
Spreading out fear
Dispelled on the way,
Without stop or stay
Adventuring we go.

Where is the City?
What is waiting ahead?
To what are we led?
Hope sounds from the height;
We shall dwell in God's sight
Onwards we go.

Who built the City
Descending from heaven?
With the gold of our skill,
With the fire of our will
We built here on earth
We brought here to birth
Man's City of God.

The Spirit in Man

In the dominion of the Father
We find being and substance
In the evolution of the world
We recognize our existence.

In the Resurrection of the Son
We perceive death's ending
In the re—animation of the earth
We discover life's meaning.

In the enlightenment of the Spirit
We are blessed with illumination
In the consolation of the light,
We are stirred with determination.

Archangels

The Archangel Michael

The sword–wielder,
The dragon–confronter,
Gathering up the true aims,
Shielding the purposes of our hearts.
He watches over the conflicts
Of the dark time,
Sending down iron courage
From the shooting stars,
Lifting the heart to see ahead
The light that overcomes in darkness.

The Archangel Uriel

In the brightness,
In the magnificence of power
Shining in the sun,
The warning sounds:
Turn from the outer to the inner,
Set the heart alight
With the flame of burning zeal
That he who comes
Be seen and known,
Light–sender,
Love–giver.

The Archangel Raphael

The guardian of mysteries,
The holder of secrets
Not yet known.
He beholds the working
Of the heavens on earth.
He reveals to human minds,
He instructs the slow of heart
In secrets of healing through Christ,
Who brought to earth
What was hidden in the heavens.

The Archangel Gabriel

The messenger from the heavens
Calls the sleepers on earth
To awaken, to listen.
The heavens have not forgotten
The distant earth.
They behold from the heights
The languishing sons of men
Awaken to the light of heaven,
Hear tidings of him who comes.

For Special Occasions

For the New-Born

The door of heaven opened
And bravely you came through.
The angels at the threshold
Sent you forth to the earth.
Sent you with your message,
Sent you with your trust,
Sent you with your purpose,
Sent you with their love.

From the hands of angels we take you,
Warming our hearts with joy.
In you we meet with intentions
Showing the way ahead.
Give us tidings of heaven,
Give us the vision of purpose,
Give us the strength of loving,
Give us our trust in God.

Baptism — a Song

With shining hearts we go,
Strong in the Father's strength,
Afire in the Son's glowing love,
Wise with the Spirit's light,
Along the pathway of earth.

With burning courage we go,
Attuned to the Father's will,
Ablaze with the aims of the Son,
Endowed with the Spirit's strength,
On the way to the world of God.

With heartfelt purpose we go,
Brave with the aims afar,
Bold with the might to become,
Fired with a great intent,
Towards the Holy City ahead.

A Birthday Song

The sun in your heart shall glow,
The stars round your head shall sound,
The moon shall uphold from below,
The earth shall give firm ground.
Holding up high your head,
Stretching your hands out wide,
Your feet surely tread,
With the grace of God to guide.

Song for Confirmation

Wayfaring,
Travelling
On life's long way.

What is known,
What is safe,
Putting away.

Persisting in hope,
Faithfully on,
We shall not stay.

Aiming at right,
Avoiding the wrong,
We fear to stray.

Where goes the road?
What is its end?
We must away.

To the City of God
Hidden ahead
We seek the way.

Sorrow shall cease,
Death be undone
If we do not stay.

The City shall glow
With God's holy peace.
We tread that way.

Arisen in light
With Christ we shall shine
At the end of that way.

Man shining in glory
Is guided by Christ
To the end of God's way.

For Those who have Died

For One who Died in the Spring

The blossoms of the cherry tree were hers
In their full flowering
When every branch was bowed,
She gathered their beauty in her hands
Carrying it hence.
The spring singing of blackbirds,
The opening of primroses,
The fragrance of gillie flowers
Were hers to take with her.
For they likewise are of the heavens,
Fading so swiftly back to the homeland
Which is that of her soul.
Thither she has faded away,
Away from the tribulation,
Away from the wasteland
To the flowering meadows of Paradise.

For One who Died Suddenly

In the hustle and bustle around
The trumpets sound
Rang out
Suddenly
Loud and clear,
Its greeting near.
"Come now!" it called,
"Come without delay!"
Vanished life's noise,
Extinguished life's woe,
She turned away to go.
Who meets her,
Who greets her?
He, the light bearer,
The life bearer,
The comforter
To realms of God leading the way.

To You, Dear Child

Your light shone in our midst,
A candle lighting up the shadows of life
With joyous hope.
The candle in our home went out,
The light withdrew.
It will shine again to us
From the heavens.
The light will illumine our ways on earth
With love given and taken.
A star of hope will rise.

For Those who have Died

Did you know the questions here
But not the answers?
At the gate to the heavens
Did they stand before you
Shining in the vision,
Gleaming in the future,
Illuminated in the heart of Christ?
Is death the new birth,
Is it the answer to the question of life on earth?
Does the future reveal the past?

Elegy on a Cat

Tell your god that we loved you,
When you stand before him.
Tell him that when you came,
A visitor to the earth,
Your beauty was upon him.
Tell him that we wondered
At his splendour of wisdom
Displayed in you.
When you came in, a visitor,
From the dark, cold night,
We took you in.
You remained our friend,
For you answered always when we spoke to you.

Death

The dead are well informed
They look ahead beyond our bounds.
On further and on further still
They gaze and they must go.
Their pilgrimage unfolds its length,
Their hostelries are planets,
And the shrine they seek the sun
Where, new-born to the universe,
They suffer a sun-change,
Becoming sunlike and like suns
Dispensing light.

Birth

From spaces far beyond
Seeking again that splendid shrine,
They shall incline themselves to earth.
It is that wondrous dreaded place
To which the heart resolves to go
To find its own, and on its own
To will and work for what shall be.
Who dwelt once in the heights of heaven
Summons unborn souls to come
To open wide the door to earth
That by the moon is set ajar,
Beckoning to urgent loves and labours.

For Human Affairs

Eternity

Where does the road wend?
Further than you can see.
Where does the stream end?
In the far–distant sea.
Where does time extend?
Into Eternity.

Greetings across the World

Said the little isle to the big isle:
    You are so far away
    By night and by day.

Said the big isle to the little isle:
    The world is so wide
    South and North to divide.

Said the little isle to the big isle:
    The stars are quite strange
    In your southern sky's range.

Said the big isle to the little isle:
    The sun illumines us all
    It shines on my wide land and on your small.

Said the little isle to the big isle:
    The hearts glow with bright love
    In the dwellers below and the dwellers above.

Forgiveness

Not on the trees of Paradise
The strangest of fruit bears seed.
It is not the apple of life nor knowledge freed.
Its seed will never scatter in that garden,
But is planted in the dark of earth
The place where Man is alone from birth.
But see, the immortal one is with him
Who knows the lonely cross,
Who withstands the fear of loss,
Who sheds unceasingly the light of grace.
The cross–tree is planted on earth
Bearing strange fruits of grace,
Stronger than the apple of strife,
Tasting of fresh, unimagined life,
The fruit of forgiveness
Both received and given.

For a Midsummer Fire

Flames flow upward
Smoke spread outward
Ash drop downward
Fire transmuting
Smoke dissolving
Ash deadening.
Flames of Spirit spring
Heavenward from human hearts.
Smoke of darkness dissolve
Into nought from human souls.
Ashes of death lie quiet —
Seed–bed of Spirit in human forms.

The Festivals

Advent

We who look ahead
Behold thee coming towards us,
Coming through the door of the clouds,
Proclaiming what is and what shall be.
Strengthen our faith,
Thou who art, who will be
Throughout the times.
Make clear our sight,
Thou who art born for what is to come.

Christmas

I went walking under a cloud.
The cloud was thick above my head.
What is beyond the cloud? I said.

I went asking from day to day
What sounds are those from out of sight?
Angels are gathering in the light.

Some came running to Bethlehem.
The heavens had opened to their sight.
Angels proclaimed the coming light.

Some went riding to Bethlehem.
The star went gliding overhead.
The light will shine on earth, they said.

I was obscured within the cloud.
Is the light lost to me? I cried.
It shines within, angels replied.

I parted the cloud and folded it.
A cloak it seemed to clothe the light.
Within the cloud the glow gleams bright.

Epiphany

What was invisible to behold,
What was unknown is known.
Open our eyes to the light of grace,
Unloose our hearts from fear,
Be with us in the strength of love,
Lead us in the hope of courage
Along the path of tribulation,
Till the overcoming is attained.

Lent

Cast down to the depths,
Raise us to uprightness.
Make us stand straight on the earth,
Head high, feet firm, hands free.
Lift us from uncertainty,
Bestow on us our humanity.
Keep us in thy faith
That we fall not away into the gloom.

Easter

Who descends into the deep?
Who plunges into death's dark?
Who penetrates the secret of sorrow,
Following the way of grief?
Who would engender compassion,
World–wide, to enfold all Mankind,
Warming likewise the single heart?

Who had the ear to hear from the heavens
The lament of human need on earth,
Rising to trouble the sons of God?

He it is, who came to the Father,
Sharing the sorrow of angels,
Grieving at the dilemma of fallen Man.
Who will bring aid to the lost brother,
Our youngest, clutched in the grip of evil?

The Father spread wide his arms,
Upholding the cross of death,
Whereon he hung, the Son,
Offering himself on the altar of the earth
To enact the mystery of redemption.

   For the death–doomed — LIFE
   For the evil–impelled — LIGHT
   For the fear–fettered — LOVE

Prayer to Man becoming Resurrected

The wayfarer is on the way.
Who points ahead?
Who gives the sign?
Who lights the way?
The beckoner,
The dark dispeller,
The light defender.

Whither wends the wayfarer?
Christ shall lead him,
Christ shall uphold him,
Christ shall befriend him,
The shepherd of sheep,
The guardian of the gate,
The guide to the City of God.

To the Ascending One

Earth could not hold,
Death not confine,
Man not compel
The God of the sun.

In light uprising,
With life death defeating,
With love dark dispelling,
Christ's sun has risen up.

Heaven sees the dawning
Light of Spirit creating,
In life resurrecting,
The sun defeats death.

Earth offers to heaven
Christ's spirit uprisen,
Man's praise shall be given
To him who ascends.

Heaven shall receive him,
Earth shall still hold him,
Man shall still know him
As the guide on the way.

Whitsun

Spirit sent from God come us–ward,
Deposit thy flame
Where the Christ–seeking heart awaits.
May light burst from the flame
Burning more courageously
From day to day.
Shedding its light of wisdom
From night to night.

Saint John's Tide

Father in the heavens
Who brought forth Man in glory,
Who guards in thy holy heart
The pattern Mankind defaces.
Look on us with compassion,
Maintain thy loving thought
That it to forgiveness ripen.

Mother on earth
Who cherished the Child of God,
Who received with care to comfort
The foundling from the heavens.
Look on us with fresh hope
Who walk the way of salvation,
Our sending to fulfil.

Son of God on earth descended,
Son of Man to God ascended,
Leading us on the sorry path
Towards our fulfilment,
Letting us not stay
Unfinished, disappointed here.
Call us from earthbound hopes
To follow thee.

To the Father in the Heights

Lift up your hearts.
Turn to the light.
It quickens the world
In beams of sun shining.

Open your hearts.
Kindle the light
That enlightens the soul
With true grace of the Father.

Receive in your hearts.
Look up to behold
The bright vision of Man
In the realms of the Father.

To the Mother in the Depths

Look down to the depths.
Know what they show
Who reveal on the earth
The true grace of the Mother.

Open your hearts.
Be strong in your trust.
The Mother will cherish
The true Child from the stars.

Drop down into flesh.
Take hold of the will.
Be human on earth
Wholly Man to become.

Michaelmas

To the Risen One

Death is undone,
Life is new come.
Waken our will,
Heart weakness heal,
Enliven the heart,
Strengthen the will.
Radiance shall prevail,
Goodwill shall avail,
Thought and deed true,
Bear witness anew.

To the Archangel

Wield the flaming sword
Guarding our honesty of heart.
Raise the beckoning hand,
Calling us to greater endeavour.
Reprove the slackening will,
Overtaken by lethargy.
Strengthen bravery of action
Threatened by lassitude.
Unveil the true vision of the Christ,
Heart inspiring, faith confirming.

To Man Resurrecting

Downcast Man rise up,
Head upheld.
Despised Man be crowned
With glory of light.
Fearful Man be bold
With heaven–sent purpose.
Wayward Man be told
The way of Christ's salvation.

Trinity

Father
We find in the depths thine image,
We find in the heights thy presence,
We know in the widths the touch of thy blessing.

Son
We heard the voice of thy word,
It sounds in the heart within,
It sounds in the heart beyond.
Listening through the world it sounds again.

Spirit
We see thy flame within,
We see thy light around,
We praise each other's flames
Illumined by the Spirit's life.

For Children:
Carols for the Festivals
of the Year

Advent

Singing stars,
Musing moon,
Tell us aright
What we hear in the night.

Clear–eyed sun,
Brightening light,
Tell us by day
What we heard them say.

Calling to the stars,
Passing their way,
At the turn of the year
He is due to appear.

Descending from the sun,
Moving with the moon,
He steps down to the earth
At the hour of his birth.

Greeting the mother,
Beckoning the father,
Son of Man he is born
For Mankind forlorn.

Christmas

"Behold," sang the stars.
Day after day
We go on our way
Without stop or stay.

"Beyond," sang the stars.
In the round that we run
A new star has begun
To descend from the sun.

"Hear," shouted the angels.
The message we sing
As hasting we wing
Our tidings to bring.

"Waken you shepherds,"
To behold with your eyes
The Child where he lies
In so humble a guise.

"Come," called the kings,
To follow the light
That illumines the night,
To comfort our plight.

Epiphany

Listen to the star
Calling from afar.
Behold his light
As the sun so bright.
Go on your way
Without delay.
On Christmas morn
The Child was born.
Bring gifts to take
For a king's sake.
To you is given
The king of heaven
Whose grace we know
Here on earth below.

Lent

Dark clouds in the sky
Blown about by harsh winds.
The world is grown cold,
The world is grown old.

Dark fears in my heart
Blown about by black thoughts.
The world seems to threaten,
The world will soon deaden.

Whence comes my strong help,
When will lighten my heart?
The sky with light glimmers,
The wind with hope murmurs.

Easter Carol

Out of the dark the rising Sun,
Out of the seed the growing grain,
Out of the pain the strength to live,
Out of death's doom
Christ risen again.

Into the light of the risen Sun,
Into the pilgrimage of grace,
Into the courage of death overcome,
Into life's promise
With Christ we are risen.

Ascension

The sun receives him,
The stars perceive him,
The moon releases him.

The angels will greet him,
The archangels will meet him,
God's servants will treat of him.

Earth will uphold him,
Mankind will still hold him,
Our eyes will behold him
As joins earth to heaven.

Whitsun

There is glory in the blossoms,
Their cup with sunlight filled.
There is glory in the heart,
In the light of Christ fulfilled.
There is glory among angels.
Who tend the human souls,
And lead through joy and sorrow
Towards high and heavenly goals.

Midsummer

Flames of fire,
High and higher,
Leaping to the light
Into heaven's might
To meet the heavens bright.
What is dark they reject,
What is light they reflect,
Ashes dropped down,
Flames forming a crown
The Earth–Mother will wear
At the heart of the year.

Michaelmas

The dragon dread
Rears his head.
The Angel strong
Comes along.
The sword of light
He wields with might.
The dragon shall go
Down below,
Down, down below.
The Angel in the Sun
With light has come,
The dark to dispel,
Ourselves to heal.

Trinity

In the singing of birds
Is the sound of God.
In the swimming of fish
Is the power of God.
In the moving of beasts
Is the willing of God.
In the heart of Man
Is the dwelling of God.

In my heart and my head,
In my hands and my feet,
God's Spirit within me
Shall move and shall speak.

Prayers and Graces

Collected by Michael Jones

This popular collection includes prayers for the expectant mother, for the child before and after birth, for one who has committed suicide, and for the soul between death and funeral.

Meditative Prayers for Today

Adam Bittleston

These prayers help to experience the rhythms of waking and sleeping, the days of the week, the seasons and festivals of the year. There are also prayers for special needs: children, illness, thanksgiving, for the dead, against fear.

Floris Books